Quilts of Chestnut Ridge

Autumn at the Courthouse

Debbie Pierce

Schiffer Publishing Ltd.

4880 Lower Valley Road, Atglen, Pennsylvania 19310

Other Schiffer Books on Related Subjects:

A Quilt Block Challenge: Vintage Revisited. Mary Kerr. ISBN: 978-0-3457-3 $24.99

Heirloom Quilt Designs for Today. Lorie Martin & Jim Burnley. ISBN: 978-0-7643-2669-1 $24.95

Fiber Expressions: The Contemporary Quilt. Quilt National. ISBN: 0-88740-093-0 $12.95

Schiffer Books are available at special discounts for bulk purchases for sales promotions or premiums. Special editions, including personalized covers, corporate imprints, and excerpts can be created in large quantities for special needs. For more information contact the publisher:

Schiffer Publishing Ltd.
4880 Lower Valley Road
Atglen, PA 19310
Phone: (610) 593-1777; Fax: (610) 593-2002
E-mail: Info@schifferbooks.com

For the largest selection of fine reference books on this and related subjects, please visit our web site at
www.schifferbooks.com

We are always looking for people to write books on new and related subjects. If you have an idea for a book please contact us at the above address.

This book may be purchased from the publisher. Include $5.00 for shipping. Please try your bookstore first. You may write for a free catalog.

In Europe, Schiffer books are distributed by
Bushwood Books
6 Marksbury Ave.
Kew Gardens
Surrey TW9 4JF England
Phone: 44 (0) 20 8392 8585; Fax: 44 (0) 20 8392 9876
E-mail: info@bushwoodbooks.co.uk
Web site: www.bushwoodbooks.co.uk

Copyright © 2011 by Debbie Pierce

Library of Congress Control Number: 2011921526

Designed by Stephanie Daugherty
Type set in Kabel Dm BT/Garamond/Zurich BT

ISBN: 978-0-7643-3699-7
Printed in China

Dedication

This book is dedicated to my mother, Elizabeth Reynolds Hilaman, and my aunt, Anna Reynolds Davis Steele, who both instilled a love of sewing in me. Some of my first memories involve Mom and my fascination with an antique Singer® treadle sewing machine. When I was about ten, Aunt Ann helped me make my first skirt. I remember passing up fishing down at the pond with my brother, sister, and cousins because I wanted to finish hemming my red calico, gathered skirt. Over thirty years later, Mom and Aunt Ann persuaded me to begin quilting. Their influence has enriched my life.

Acknowledgements

I would like to thank those who made this book possible:

Nancy Schiffer, my editor, for answering my many questions

Jeff Snyder for his photography expertise

Jordan Carlson, my son-in-law, for his assistance and patience with all my computer issues

Jeannie Mullins and Phyllis Deel for arranging my first quilting classes

The Southern Highland Craft Guild for helping us market our creations

All my quilting students. I have learned just as much from them!

My children: Sherry, Robby, Michelle, Melody, Amy, and Michael, who were the motivating force behind Chestnut Ridge Quilting

Clancy, my husband, for his encouragement and tolerance of my "quilting addiction"

And finally, my Lord Jesus Christ. Nothing is impossible to achieve if you allow God to show you how to do it and trust in Him.

Contents

I started quilting "under protest." My mother had a Dahlia quilt top from an auction in Lancaster County, Pennsylvania, and my Aunt Ann had a quilting frame. Together they decided that my children, then ages five to eleven, and I should finish this quilt. I resisted and said that it would take too long. In the end they persuaded us to take on the project.

We set up the 8-by-10-foot frame in our living room. My husband could barely make it to his favorite chair! It took us about a year to finish, and by then the children and I could not imagine life without quilting. We were hooked! I was going to have to learn to piece quilts.

I went to the Lee County Public Library and checked out *Quilts! Quilts!! Quilts!!! The Complete Guide to Quiltmaking*, by Diana McClun and Laura Nownes. Upon seeing the Star of Bethlehem quilt, I just **had** to make one. For practice, I started with a Fence Rail quilt. Next, I made a Sawtooth Star, then the Star of Bethlehem. By this time, the children wanted to piece quilts, too!

When my Aunt Ann learned that we were all quilting, she gave us a 1958, straight-stitch, Singer® sewing machine, Model 403A. It had been in the family since it was new, had not been used for quite a while, and desperately needed servicing. My boys, Robby and Michael, took on the challenge and, following the instructions in the owner's manual, got it into excellent working order. From then on it was the only machine any of us wanted to use. We later found a Model

6

Our first quilt.

404 at a flea market and added it to our fleet. I still use these machines for all my piecing, since they make such nice stitches and are so reliable.

In our area of the Appalachian Mountains, there were several cooperatives to assist in marketing traditional crafts. The children and I made an assortment of quilts, wall hangings, coasters, and tote bags to submit. Shortly, Chestnut Ridge Quilting was born. We set up a sewing room in our home and started production. Our creations sold very well and the children started contemplating how they would use their earnings.

Amy, then twelve, decided she wanted a horse. We already had a barn and a fenced pasture. My husband, Clancy, told her that she could have a horse after she had saved enough for the initial purchase and related expenses for a year. In addition, she would be responsible for all the care. Two years later, Amy brought home her long-awaited horse.

Melody chose to raise Boer goats with her quilting money. Over the years her herd grew. She kept the nannies and sold the billies. Eventually, she sold the whole herd and purchased a car with her profits. Michael, continued to do the maintenance on our sewing machines and went on to become a mechanic.

Robby was interested in tennis and used his money for tennis equipment and tournaments. He competed in the USTA regional youth competitions and received a full, tennis scholarship to Virginia Intermont College.

While attending college, spending money continued to be earned through quilting. The children sewed at home while on breaks and sometimes took hand work back to school to be completed. Michelle went on to receive a B. S. in Business Administration from Berea College.

All quilts in this book have been designed, pieced, and hand quilted by Chestnut Ridge Quilting.

aking a quilt is much like putting a puzzle together, but you have to make the pieces first. Making those pieces in an efficient, accurate manner is the subject of this book.

Autumn at the Courthouse is the combination of two traditional quilt blocks: *Autumn Leaf* and *Courthouse Steps*. These blocks will be presented along with step-by-step instructions and photographs of the steps. **Be sure to read all the instructions before beginning**.

Although the results look traditional, the block are achieved through non-traditional method.

The *Autumn Leaf* blocks will have extr background fabric around the edges and wi be trimmed to the proper size. This makes much easier to keep from losing the point on the leaves. While sewing these blocks, kee in mind that the outer edges will be trimme away, and therefore do not need to be ever Instead, concentrate on matching the inne seam lines.

The *Courthouse Steps* blocks that are used toward the center of the quilt will be whole blocks and those used around the edge will be half or quarter blocks. This not only makes for less work in piecing, it also yields more accurate results and less fabric waste.

It is essential to pay close attention to the size of the pressed block as it is constructed. If it is too large or too small, you will be able to tell when trimming, since all blocks will be trimmed to whole inch measures.

Use one light background fabric and a variety of dark fabrics. The more dark fabrics used, the better the results. This is a good opportunity to use up leftover scraps and strips. Since contrast is desired between the light and dark areas, it is best to avoid medium-value fabrics.

The quilts presented have 7½" blocks. Any 7 ½" block with a neutral background could be substituted for the Autumn Leaf block. Additionally, a 10 ½" variation can be created by adding an extra round of "logs" on the Courthouse Steps blocks. Examples of my variations are shown in the Gallery at the end of the book.

Every quilt is unique, a one-of-a kind work of art. Even when the same pattern is used, the resulting quilts vary widely, taking on the style of its creator. Allow your own preferences to guide your fabric choices. Take the ideas presented in this book and adapt them to create your own variations. There is no limit to the designs that are possible!

Supplies and Equipment

It is not the purpose of this book to include all aspects of quilting, since there are many excellent and complete quiltmaking books already available. I suggest that this book be used in conjunction with a general quilt book. My personal favorite is *Quilts! Quilts!! Quilts!!! The*

Complete Guide to Quiltmaking, by Diana McClu and Laura Nownes.

Your sewing machine will affect the quali of the quilts you produce. It must maintai proper tension to achieve smooth seams. I st prefer my 1958 Singer straight stitch.

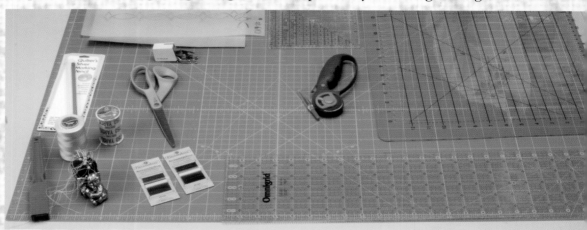

Supplies for all steps. Sewing machine, walking foot, cotton fabrics, 6" x 24" plastic ruler, June Taylor Shape Cut™ ruler, 6 ½" square ruler with 45° line, rotary cutter and mat, seam ripper, straight pins, scissors, neutral cotton machine thread, hand-quilting thread, hand-quilting needles, quilting stencils, quilter's silver marking pencil, pencil sharpener, sandpaper, quilter's safety pins, and quilting hoop.

Courthouse Steps Blocks and Variations

The *Courthouse Steps* block is a *Log Cabin* variation. For this quilt, it is used to create a frame around the *Autumn Leaf* and the illusion of a diagonal setting.

For each *Courthouse Steps* block, you will need the center square and 2" strips of fabric. The placement of the light and dark fabrics creates the pattern.

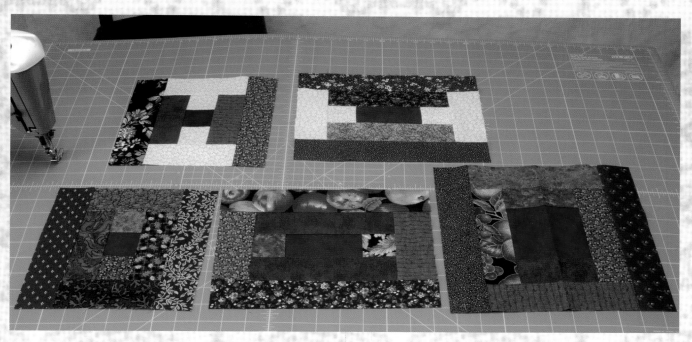

These are the five types of Courthouse Steps blocks. Clockwise from upper left: CS2x2, CS2x4, D4x4, D2x4, and D2x2. The Courthouse Steps (CS) blocks are half light, half dark. The Dark (D) blocks are all dark. The numbers (2x2, 2x4, and 4x4) refer to the size of the center in inches.

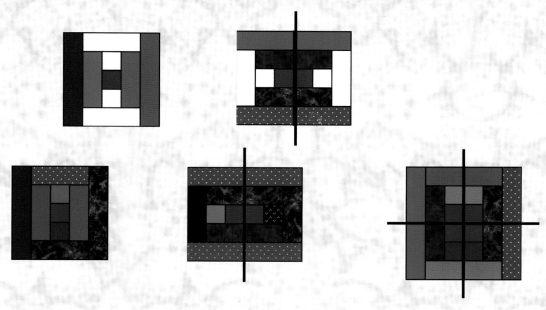

General Instructions for *CS* 2x2, 7 ½" Finished size

Lay out fabric with four thickness. The center fold of the fabric must be parallel to the selvages. When using the Shape Cut™ ruler it is not necessary to align fabric with lines on mat.

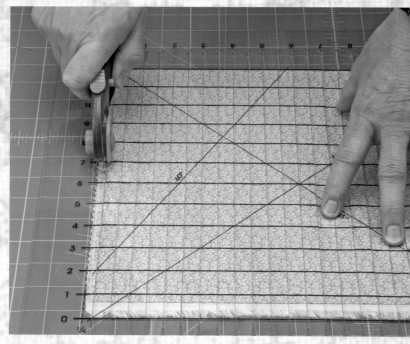

Place the ruler squarely on the fabric and trim raw edges. Notice that the ruler marking is placed on the fold of the fabric. For straight strips, the fabric must be folded squarely and the ruler accurately placed.

Without moving ruler, cut two inch strips.

To cut 2" squares, first cut strips. Rotate ruler 90° and cut at 2" intervals. Always align ruler squarely with edge of fabric.

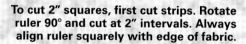

Choose one light background fabric and a variety of dark fabrics for the "log" fabrics. Use leftover scraps and as many different fabrics as possible. Shown are light background, greens, blues, purples, and bold prints that I classify as "zingers."

Block centers 2" x 2", 2" x 4", and 4" x 4". The size of the block center will vary according to the type of block being made.

Lay first strip to be joined to center right side up. One by one lay centers on top leaving about ¼" between centers and join in a scant ¼" seam. Continue until all centers have been joined. Note: My definition of a scant ¼" seam is two threads short of ¼". Be sure that the seam allowance used allows for slight trimming so that the finished blocks are accurate.

First press flat without sliding the iron. Hint: Position the fabric on top that the seam allowance will be pressed toward.

Press seam allowance away from center. Slide the side of the iron into the fold being careful to avoid "accordion" folds. All Courthouse Steps seam allowances will be pressed away from the center.

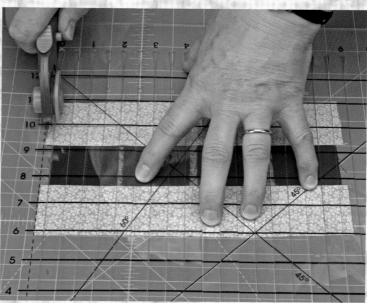

Using the shape cut ruler, trim strips to the same size as centers. All trimming will be in whole inch measurements.

Join the opposite side of center unit to a strip placed right side up. Press.

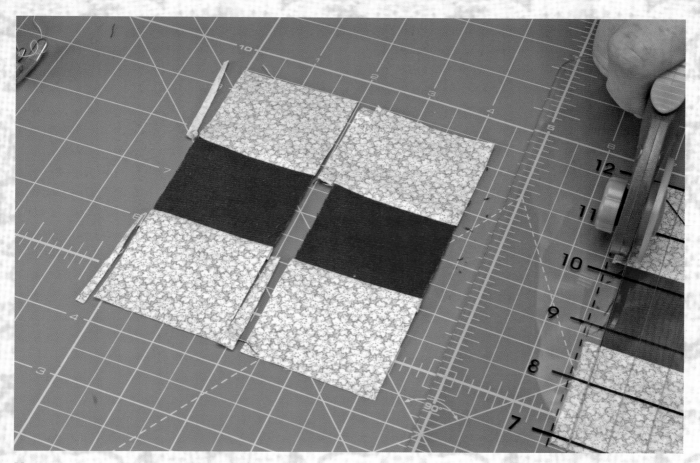

Move ruler to match each center square.

An alternate method for large numbers of blocks is to sew background strips to both sides of a 2" center strip, then cut into two-inch sections.

Continue the same process with strips to be joined right side up. Lay previous unit on top and stitch. When adding dark strips, change to a different fabric frequently to achieve a "scrappy" effect.

Join dark fabrics to both sides.

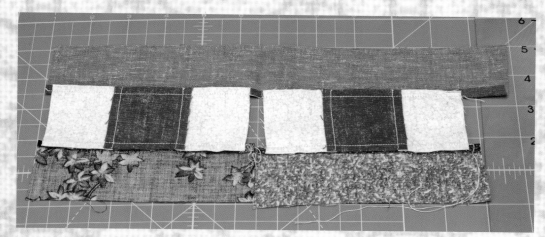

Seams are pressed away from the center square.

Trim to 5". Note the small amount of fabric trimmed from sides of the block. This assures that the block is the correct size. If the block is too small, then adjust the seam allowance on the next round of strips to make it larger.

Continue same process with strips to be joined right side up. Repeat on both sides.

Trim block in both directions to 8" square.

Courthouse Steps Variations

CS 2x4

For Courthouse Step blocks with a 2" x 4" center (CS2x4), first join background fabric to the 2" sides.

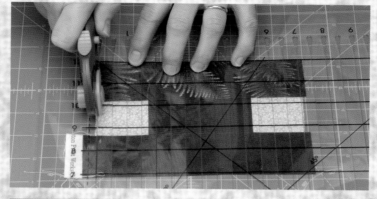

Proceed as with CS2x2 blocks.

Trim in both directions to 8" x 10".

Here's the trimmed 8" x 10" block.

Now cut it in half crosswise.

All Dark *Courthouse Steps* Blocks
a
D2x2, D2x4, and D4x4

To make the dark blocks, repeat the process with all dark strips. Shown are D2x2 and D2x4. The D2x4 blocks will be cut in half crosswise to form edge blocks.

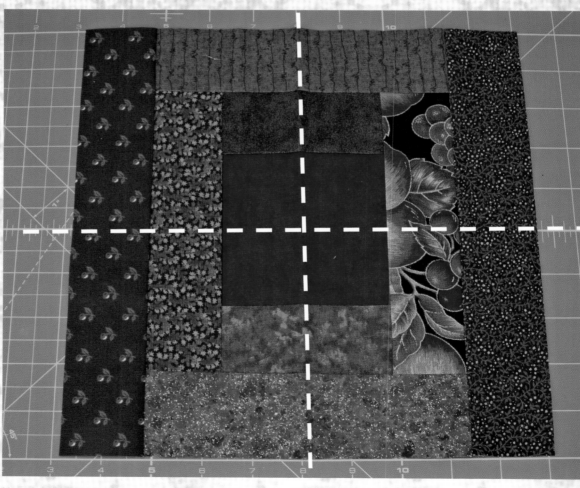

Here is a D4x4 block, trimmed to 10" x 10".
It will be cut into quarters to form the four corner blocks.

Autumn Leaf Block
7 ½" Finished size

The *Autumn Leaf* is a striking block that can be made to resemble a leaf changing color. This effect is achieved by fabric selection and placement. I choose bold, jewel-tone fabrics. It works well to use one larger print, a "zinger" in each leaf. For each block choose four "leaf" fabrics, one light-colored background fabric, and a "stem" fabric.

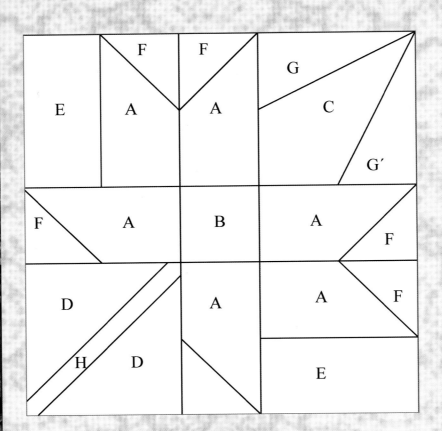

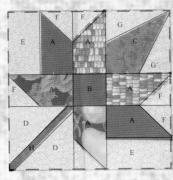

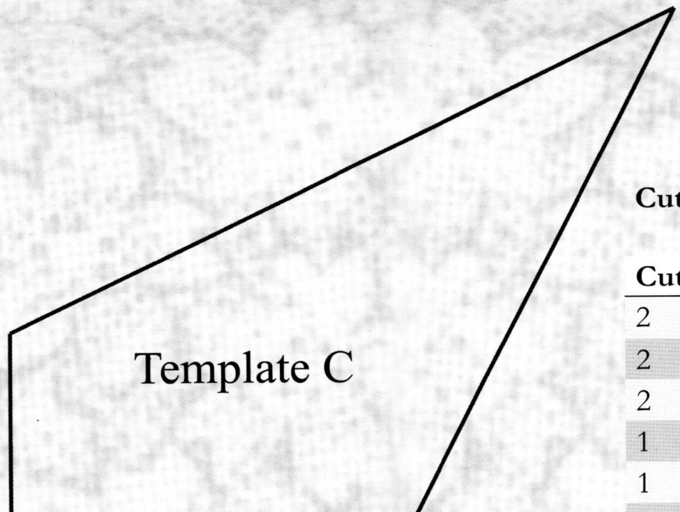

Template C

Cut the following for each leaf:

Cut	Leaf	Fabric	Size
2	A	#1	2" x 3 ½"
2	A	#2	2" x 3 ½"
2	A	#3	2" x 3 ½"
1	B	#2	2" x 2"
1	C	#4	3 ½" x 3 ½"

Trim to form kite, Template C

Cut Background			
1	D	4" x 4"	Cut diagonally
2	E	2 ½" x 4"	
6	F	2" x 2½"	
2	G	4 ¾" x 2 ½"	Cut diagonally with wrong sides together

Cut Stem			
1	H	¾" x 6"	

Use a ¼-inch seam allowance throughout.
Press all seams toward leaf fabrics.

24

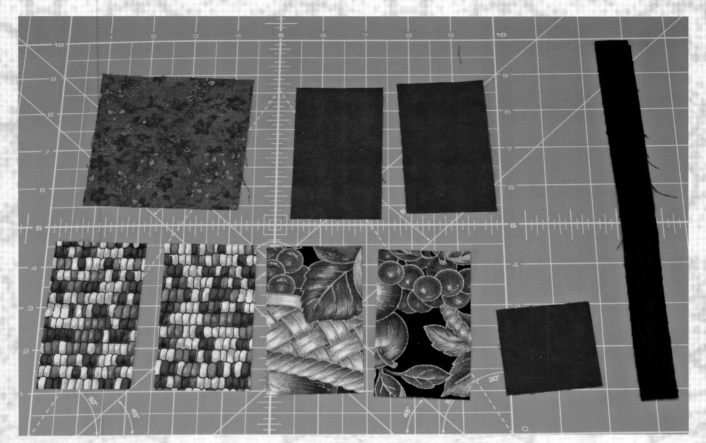

Choose
coordinating
leaf fabrics.
These are my
fabrics for
one leaf.

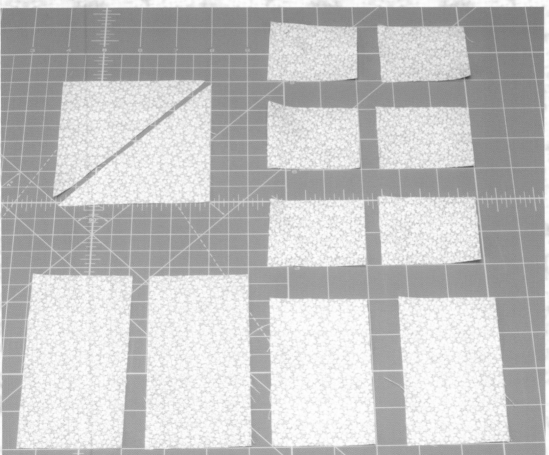

Background pieces
for one leaf.

Trim leaf tip C to form kite. Cut from one corner to center of opposite sides (1 3/4"), or trim to Template C

Cut D and G background diagonally. Leave the two G pieces wrong sides together while cutting to form G reversed pieces (G´).

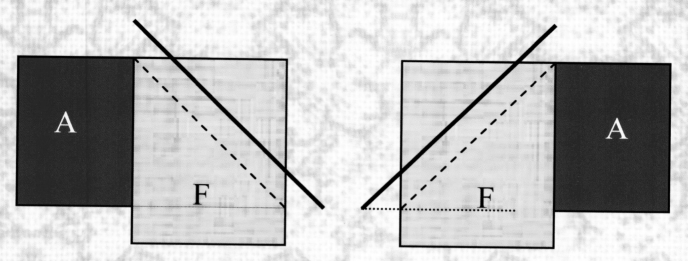

Stitch diagonally (dotted line), then trim seam allowance to ¼" (solid line).

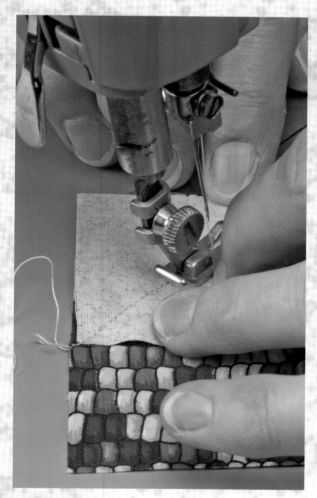

Join A-F units. Half of the units must be reversed, so alternately join an F piece to the right end and then to the left end of the A pieces as shown. Match the sides and corners, then begin and end stitching where the two fabrics intersect. Draw the stitching line if needed.

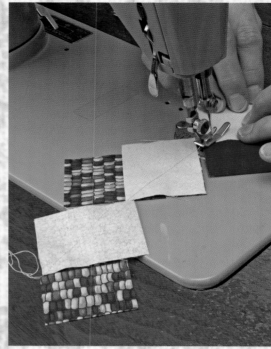

Like so.

Trim seam allowance to ¼".

Press seam allowance toward leaf fabric.

Join C-G unit. Use a scant ¼" seam. There will be a little V that forms when the edges are aligned. Start stitching in the V.

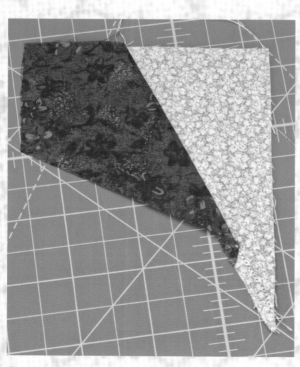

Press seam toward leaf fabric.

Trim extra seam allowance as shown.

Lay kite on top of background fabric, align edges, and start to stitch in the V. Press seam allowances toward leaf fabric. Always press toward the leaf fabric!

Note that the outside edges may not match up. They will be trimmed later.

Join D-H unit using a scant ¼" seam.

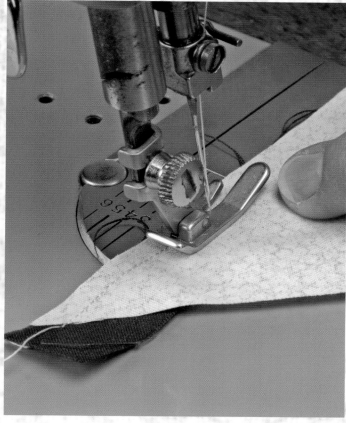

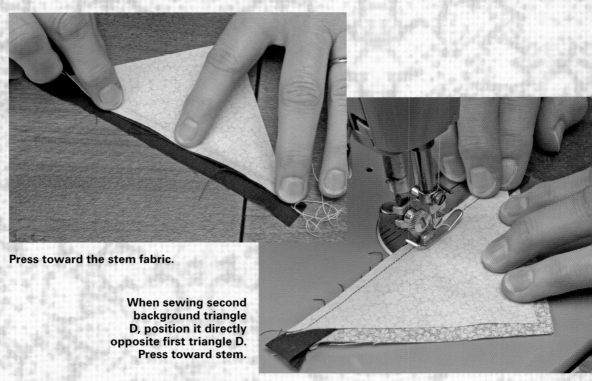

Press toward the stem fabric.

When sewing second background triangle D, position it directly opposite first triangle D. Press toward stem.

Finished D-H unit.

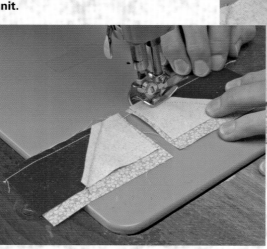

Join E to A-F units along longest dark side as shown. Press.

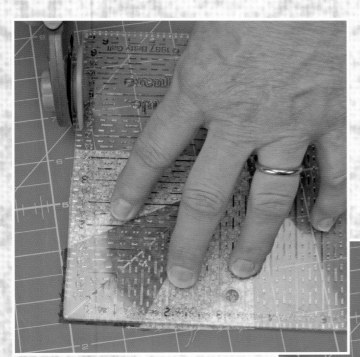

Square inner corners of DH and CG units.

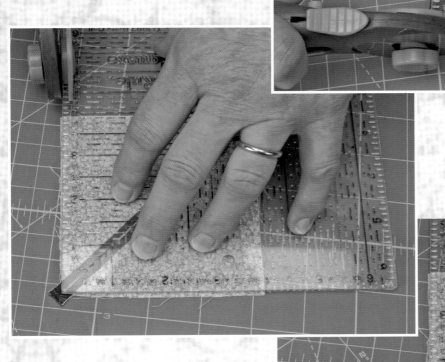

Lay out the pieces to form a leaf. If necessary, lay the pieces on top of the leaf picture on page 23.

Flip middle row over the row on the left (when facing you).

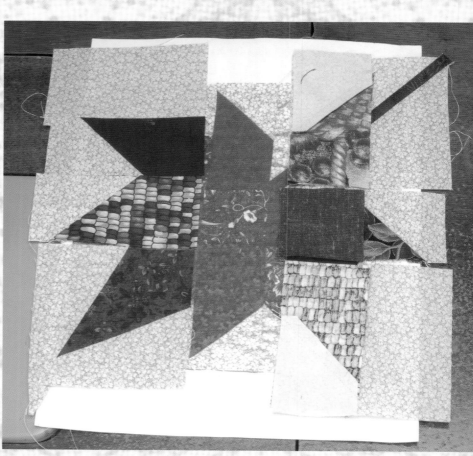

Start sewing the flipped sections together, beginning in the top left. Do not cut the thread between sections! This keeps the pieces in the correct position.

The inner edges of the leaf need to be even. The outer edges will be trimmed later.

Moving on to the middle section.

Sewing the bottom
section now.

The left and middle
sections are now
sewn together. Do
not cut apart.

The inner edges
need to match.
Outer edges may
not match and
that's all right.

Now it is time to attach the right hand units. Flip them over on top of the center units before sewing. Notice that the leaf tip has been aligned with the inner edge, not the outer edge of the block. The excess will be trimmed when finished.

All the sections are now sewn together. Do not cut thread joining units.

Press the seams toward the darker fabric.

Alternate the seams in the center as shown.

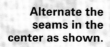

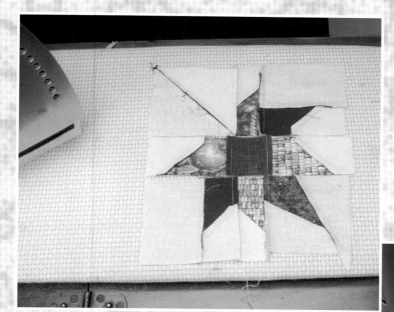

The seams are now pressed and going in the directions they should go. Do not cut apart.

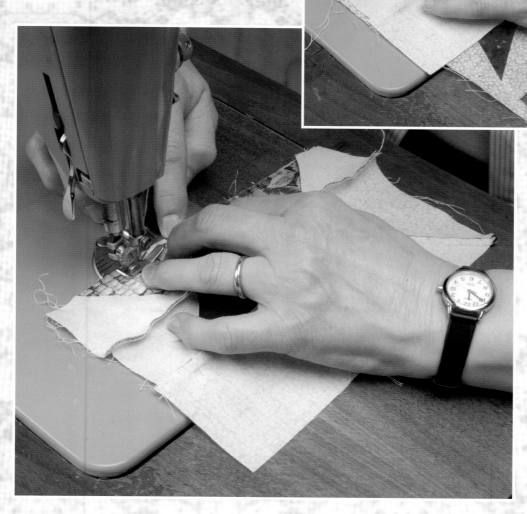

Match the inner seams and stitch the remaining seam lines, matching centers. Pin if necessary. Note: The outside edges do not need to match at this time.

Stitch the remaining seam. You can pin if necessary.

All the seams are now stitched and pressed.

Position Shape Cut™ ruler so 45 degree line goes up through stem and tip of the leaf. Adjust to have at least ¼" of background outside every leaf tip. The block will be trimmed to 8" square.

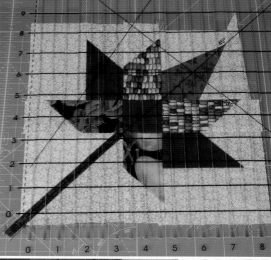

Begin trimming sides. Cut at 0 and 8 inches.

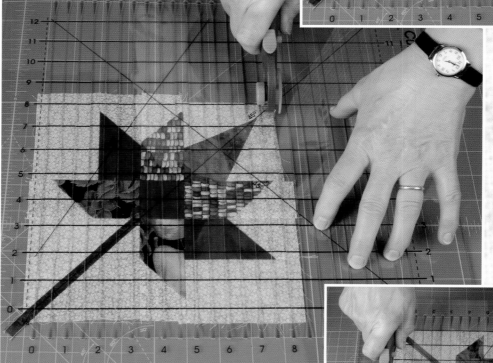

Rotate the leaf 90°, realign the Shape Cut™ ruler, and cut the other two sides.

Finishing the Quilt

Autumn at the Courthouse, 22"x 22"

These are the finished and trimmed blocks for a one-leaf *Autumn at the Courthouse* wall hanging. Now we will join them together to make a wall hanging.

Arrange the blocks, adjusting positions, until you find a pleasing arrangement. Note that all the red squares are around the outside.

As when joining the leaf units, flip the center blocks to the left, matching the inside edges.

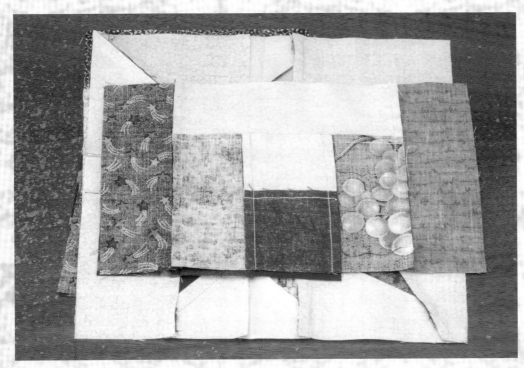

When working with a larger piece, next stack the pieces in order with the upper left on top.

Sew the seams of all three pieces in sequence, checking to be sure the block placement is correct. Do not cut the threads in between.

The first seam is sewn.

44

Attach remaining pieces, making sure that the pattern is correct. Again, do not cut the connecting threads.

Press the seams in the middle section away from the leaf. The remaining seams are pressed toward the center.

Do not cut the pieces apart.

Sew the remaining two seams.

The seams are all sewn. Press the last two seams away from the center leaf.

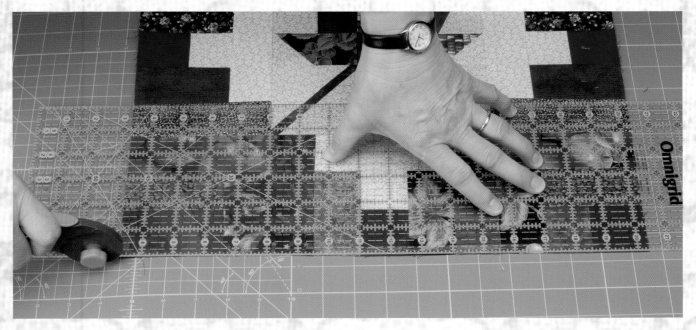

Straighten the edges.

Adding the Borders

Now it is time to choose a border. Try different fabrics to see what you feel works best.

Add the side borders first. Notice that the end of the border strip extends beyond the edge.

Press, then trim ever

Add the remaining borders. Press again.

Trim the corners

Marking

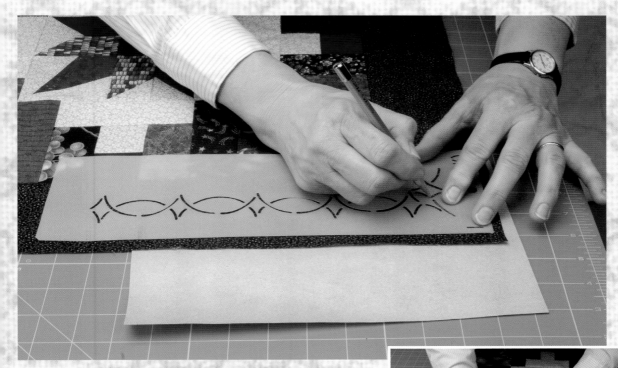

I will be hand quilting the wall hanging. The inner blocks are going to be quilted "in the ditch" and will not require any marking. Here, the border is being marked using a stencil and silver quilting pencil. Use sandpaper underneath to keep the cloth from slipping. This quilting pattern can be lengthened or shortened in the middle of the arcs to fit any size border.

Continue to stencil around the border.

The border has been marked. If desired this step can be delayed until just before the border is quilted.

Basting

To layer the wall hanging, first smooth out the backing fabric and clamp it without stretching. Do the same with the batting and the top.

The three layers of the wall hanging will be pinned together with quilting safety pins. An alternate method would be to hand baste the layers together about every four inches using long, running stitches.

The quilt is now pinned together.

Hand Quilting

Carefully place the quilt in a hoop. Begin quilting near the center and work outward. Quilt using quilting needles (betweens) and hand quilting thread. A 10" hoop is shown.

First, the knot is hidden between the layers.

Quilt along all seam lines "in the ditch". The ditch is the thinner side of the seam line with no seam allowance. This makes it easier to make stitches. Rotate the end of the needle up and down while controlling the tension with a hand underneath. Make small, even stitches through all three layers. Finish off the ends by making a knot about ¼" from the quilt, then insert the needle beside the last stitch and hide the knot between the layers.

The quilting has been completed. Suggestion: Before quilting the border design machine stitch through all three layers 1/8" from the outside edge using a walking foot. This will make it easier to quilt the border.

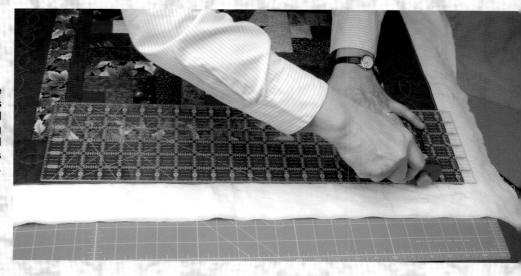

Trim the excess batting and backing after all quilting is completed.

Binding, Hanging Sleeve, and Signing

Join 2" binding strips at a 45 degree angle. Begin and end stitching where the strips meet in a V. One strip will cover about 40" around the edge. Divide the edge length by 40 to determine the total number of strips needed.

Three strips are being joined here. Trim seam allowance to ¼".

Press seam allowances open.

Press the binding strips in half, right sides together.

It is time to sew on the binding. First, run the binding around the edge of the quilt to make sure you don't have to turn a corner on a seam in the binding. This is difficult as the material gets too thick. Begin stitching 12" from the beginning of the strip. This unsewn part will be joined later.

Using a ¼" seam allowance and a walking foot, stitch to within ¼" of the corner and back stitch.

Fold the binding up at the corner at a 45 degree angle. The raw edges of the binding and the wall hanging should form a straight line.

Fold binding down with the raw edges even and the fold at the top as shown.

Stitch the next side using a ¼" seam allowance. Continue for all sides and corners. Stop 12" from starting point.

Now join the two ends of the binding. Smooth out the initial, loose end of the binding. In the center of the opening, cut a 45° slit into the top layer only of the binding strip as shown.

Unfold the binding strip and finish cutting through the strip at a 45° angle.

The finished cut
should look like this.

Smooth the other
loose end down
over the previous
cut without
stretching.

Make a 45° slit ½" past the previous cut, top layer only. Unfold the binding strip to finish the 45° cut. The two ends will overlap ½".

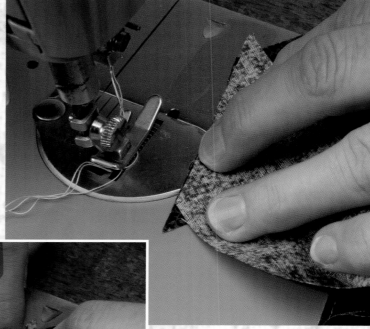

Place the ends of the binding together so they overlap ¼" from the raw edges and stitch a ¼" seam.

Press the resulting seam open.

Now finish sewing
the binding in place.

To make a hanging sleeve, cut a 5" strip of backing fabric the width of the quilt. Fold ¼" over twice, press, and stitch to form a hem on each end. Note: Hanging sleeve width must vary according to rod width.

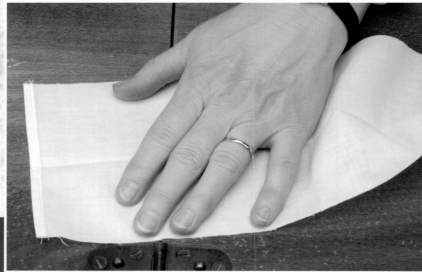

Press the hanging sleeve in half lengthwise. Center the sleeve along the top matching raw edges. Machine baste 1/8" from the edge using a walking foot.

Use matching hand quilting thread to stitch the binding onto the back.

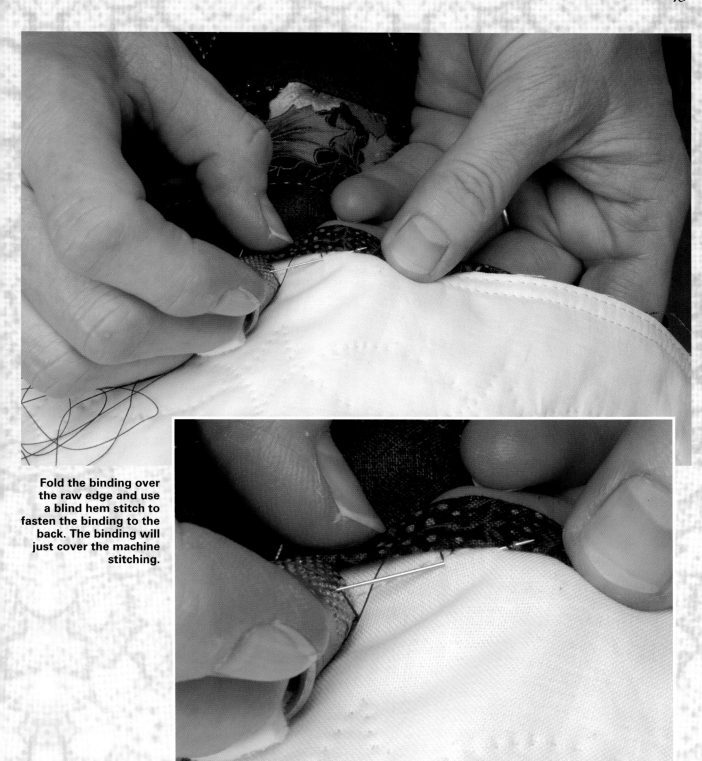

Fold the binding over the raw edge and use a blind hem stitch to fasten the binding to the back. The binding will just cover the machine stitching.

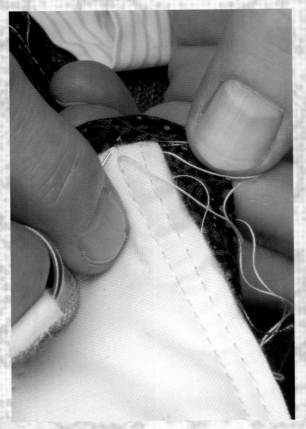

Stitch to the corner.

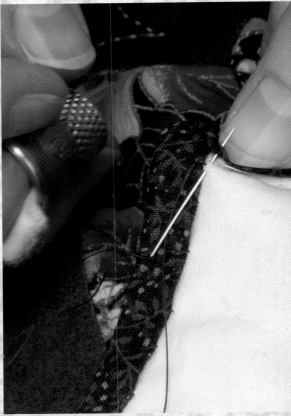

As the binding is folded, a miter will form at the corner. Take a couple extra stitches to secure the corner, then continue stitching.

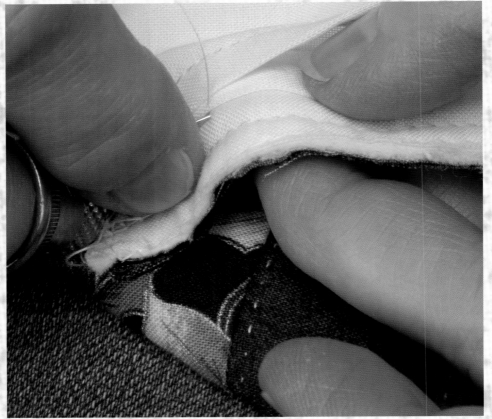

Hem inner edge of hanging sleeve to the backing of the quilt along the three loose sides. Make a label for the quilt by signing and dating a small piece of backing fabric laid on sandpaper. Use a sharp, permanent marker. Hand stitch to the back

The completed 22" x 22" *Autumn at the Courthouse* wall quilt.

Autumn at the Courthouse, 75" x 94"

Autumn at the Courthouse

	Wall	Wall	Wall/Lap	Twin	Full/Queen	King
Finished size (inches)	22x22	41x41	59x59	75x94	90x108	108x108
Leaf blocks set	1	2x2	3x3	4x5	5x6	6x6
Blocks						
Leaf	1	4	9	20	30	36
CS2x2	—	4	12	31	49	60
CS2X4	2	4	6	9	11	12
D2X2	—	1	4	12	20	25
D2X4	—	2	4	7	9	10
D4X4	1	1	1	1	1	1
Fabric (in yards)						
Red	1/8	1/8	1/8	1/4	1/2	1/2
Light background	1/4	5/8	1 1/4	2 5/8	4 1/4	4 7/8
Dark scraps	3/8	1 1/8	2 1/2	5 1/8	7 5/8	9
Stem fabric	scrap	scrap	1/8	1/8	1/8	1/4
Border #1*	1/2	1/4	1 1/2	2 1/2	2 3/4	3
Border #2	—	1/4	1 1/2	2 1/2	2 3/4	3
Border #3*	—	1/2	1 3/4	2 1/2	2 3/4	3 1/4
Cutting						
Leaf blocks						
Dark scraps						
A 2" x 3 1/2"	6	24	54	120	180	216
B 2" x 2"	1	4	9	20	30	36
C** 3 1/2" x 3 1/2"	1	4	9	20	30	36
Light background						
D*** 4" x 4"	1	4	9	20	30	36
E 2 1/2" x 4"	2	8	18	40	60	72
F 2" x 2 1/2"	6	24	54	120	180	216
G*** 4 3/4" x 2 1/2"	2	4	10	20	30	36
Stem						
H 3/4" x 6"	1	4	9	20	30	36
Courthouse Steps blocks						
Red						
2" x 2"	—	5	16	43	69	85
2" x 4"	2	6	10	16	20	22
4" x 4"	1	1	1	1	1	1
Light background						
2" strips	1	4	9	21	31	36
Dark scraps						
2" strips	4	16	36	80	120	144
Borders Cut width in inches						
Border #1	3 1/2	1 1/2	1 1/2	1 1/2	1 1/2	1 1/2
Border #2	—	2	2	2	2	2
Border #3	—	3 1/2	3 1/2	5	6 1/2	6 1/2

* If borders #1 and #3 are cut from the same fabric, only the yardage for border #3 will be required.

** Trim to form kite, Template C (See Page 24)

*** Cut in half diagonally, wrong sides together

Refer to pages 13-40 for construction of *Autumn Leaf*, CS2x4, and D4x4 blocks.

CS2x2

CS2x4 Cut in half.

D2x2

D2x4 Cut in half.

D4x4   **Cut in fourths.**

Autumn Leaf

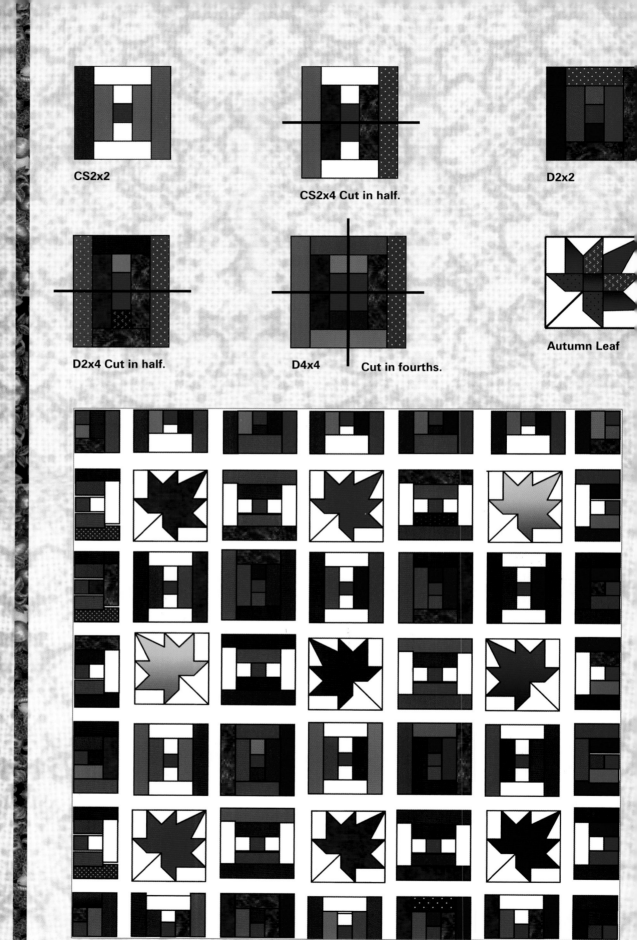

Autumn at the Courthouse **Block Layout**

Wall	Wall	Wall/Lap	Twin	Full/Queen	King
22x22	41x41	59x59	75x94	90x108	108x108

L = Leaf block, D = D2x2. The other blocks in the body of the quilt are CS2x2.
The corners are D4x4 (cut in fourths) and the edges are CS2x4 and D2x4 (cut in half).

Autumn at the Courthouse with additional borders, 27" x 27"

Autumn at the Courthouse wall quilt, 41" x 41"

Autumn at the Courthouse wall/lap quilt, 59" x 59"

Full/Queen *Autumn at the Courthouse* **quilt top, 90" x 108"**

Woodland Frolic is another combination of *Courthouse Steps* and *Autumn Leaf* blocks. In the center of the quilt, the *Autumn Leaf* blocks are surrounded by sash and multi-color posts. The sash matches the background fabric. The *Courthouse Steps* border is formed of *CS2x4* and *D4x4* blocks separated by two inch strips.

Woodland Frolic wall quilt, 43" x 43".

	Wall	Twin	Full/Queen	King
Finished size	43"x43"	74"x92"	92"x110"	110"x110"
Leaf set	3 x 3	6 x 8	8 x 10	10 x 10
Blocks				
Leaves	9	48	80	100
CS2x4	6	14	18	20
D4x4	1	1	1	1
Fabric (in yards)				
Light background	1 ¼	5 ⅛	8 ½	10
Dark scraps	1	3 ⅛	5 ¼	6 ¼
Red	⅛	⅛	⅛	⅛
Stem fabric	⅛	¼	⅜	½
Border	1 ¼	2 ⅜	3	3 ¼
Cutting				
Leaves				
Dark scraps				
A 2" x 3 ½"	54	288	480	600
B 2" x 2"	9	48	80	100
C* 3 ½" x 3 ½"	9	48	80	100
Light background				
D** 4" x 4"	9	48	80	100
E 2 ½" x 4"	18	96	160	200
F 2" x 2 ½"	54	288	480	600
G** 4 3/4" x 2 ½"	10	48	80	100
Stem				
H 3/4" x 6"	9	48	80	100
Courthouse Steps blocks				
Red				
2" x 4"	6	14	18	20
4" x 4"	1	1	1	1
Light background				
2" strips	3	7	9	10
Dark scraps				
2" strips	8	16	20	22
2" x 5"	16	32	40	44
Sash				
Light background				
2" x 8"	24	110	178	220
Posts				
Dark scraps				
2" x 2"	16	63	99	121
Border (Cut width in inches)				
	3	5 ½	5 ½	5 ½

* Trim to form kite, Template C (see page 24)

** Cut in half diagonally, wrong sides together

    Refer to pages 13-40 for construction of *Autumn Leaf*, CS2x4, and D4x4 blocks.

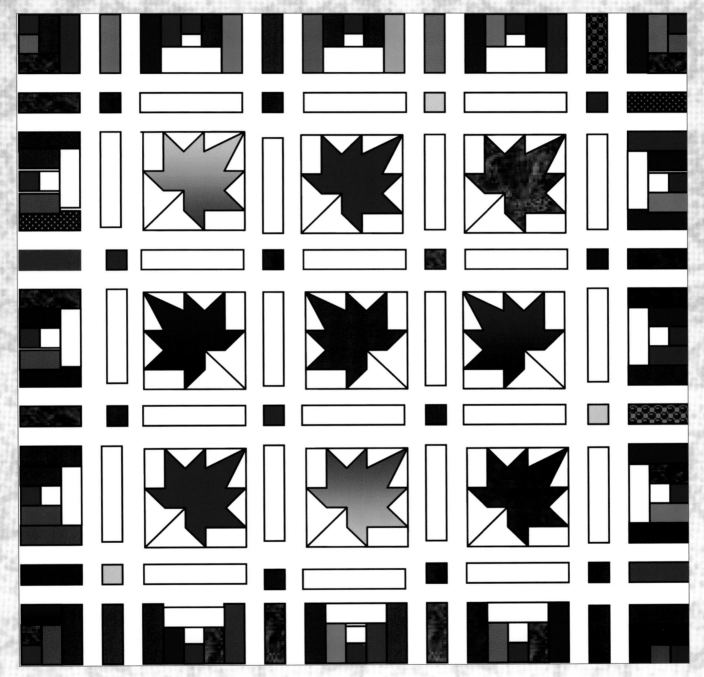

Woodland Frolic Block Layout

Autumn *Leaf* blocks can be combined with sash and posts to make wall hangings or runners. Shown are one-leaf, three-leaf, and 6-leaf. They can also be joined to form a quilt similar to *Woodland Frolic* with straight borders.

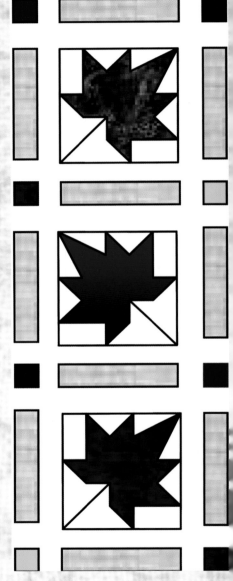

***Autumn Leaf* Wall Hanging Block Layout**

Finished size	15"x15"	15"x 33"	15"x 61"
Leaf blocks	1	3	6
Fabric			
Light background	¼	³⁄₈	½
Dark scraps	⅛	¼	³⁄₈
Sash	⅛	¼	3/8
Stem fabric	scrap	scrap	⅛
Border	¼	¼	1 ⁵⁄₈
Cutting			
Leaves			
Dark scraps			
A 2" x 3 ½"	6	18	36
B 2" x 2"	1	3	6
C* 3 ½" x 3 ½"	1	3	6
Light background			
D** 4" x 4"	1	3	6
E 2 ½" x 4"	2	6	12
F 2" x 2 ½"	6	18	36
G** 4 ¾" x 2 ½"	2	3	6
Stem			
H ¾" x 6"	1	3	6
Sash			
2" x 8"	4	10	19
Posts			
Dark scraps			
2" x 2"	4	8	14
Border (Cut width in inches)			
	2 ½	2 ½	2 ½

* Trim to form kite, Template C (See Page 24)

** Cut in half diagonally, wrong sides together

Refer to pages 23-40 for construction of *Autumn Leaf* blocks.

Autumn Leaf **wall hanging/runner, 15" x 33".**

Autumn Leaf wall hanging, 15" x 15"

Autumn Leaf runner,
15" x 61"

Courthouse Quilt Variations

Lilies at the Courthouse

Courthouse Steps blocks and 7 ½" **Carolina Lily** blocks.

One more round of "logs" was added to the *Courthouse Steps* blocks to create 10 ½" blocks. The *Carolina Lilies* are 10 ½".

One inch logs (cut 1 ½") and a two inch center square (cut 2 ½") are used to make 12" *Courthouse Steps* blocks. The *Carolina Lily* is 12".

Stars at the Courthouse

These quilts use 10 ½" *Courthouse Steps* and 10 ½" *Sawtooth Star* blocks.

86

Log Cabin

This is the scrap quilt that inspired *Autumn at the Courthouse*. I had cut my leftover fabric into 2" strips to make a scrap *Log Cabin*. About the same time I was making *Autumn Leaf* wall quilts. At two o'clock one morning, I awoke with the idea that since they were the same size, I could use the *Courthouse Steps* variation of *Log Cabin* to frame the *Autumn Leaf* blocks.

Log Cabin Barnraising, 55" x 55"

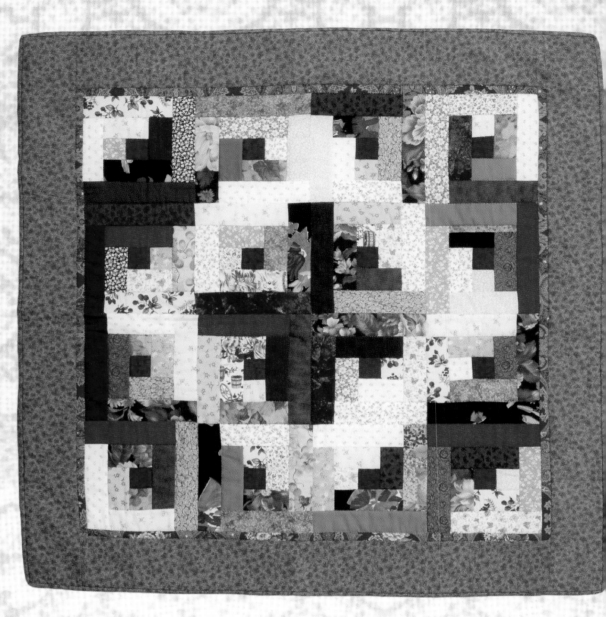

Log Cabin Barnraising, 40" x 40".

Bargello, Book Marks.

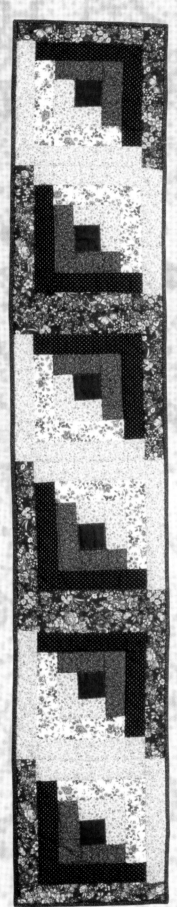

Log Cabin **Runner, 11" x 63"**

Log Cabin,
Tote Bag.

Autumn Leaf,
Tote Bag.

Demonstrations

Demonstration at Moses Cone Manor on the Blue Ridge Parkway, Blowing Rock, North Carolina

Amy, Michelle, and Sherry at Hodgson Craft Show

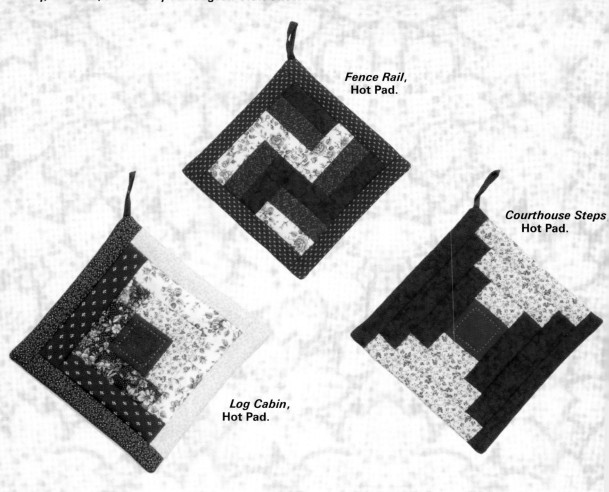

Fence Rail,
Hot Pad.

Courthouse Steps,
Hot Pad.

Log Cabin,
Hot Pad.

Demonstration at The Folk Art Center, Asheville, North Carolina

Debbie Pierce is a self-taught quilter and quilting instructor who creates traditional quilts with her own "twist." She began quilting while living on her 25-acre farm on Chestnut Ridge in the hills of Lee County, Virginia. She and her six, home-schooled children established Chestnut Ridge Quilting in 1996 to produce and market their quilted creations. In 2003 she was accepted into the Southern Highland Craft Guild.

Debbie loves to share her unique insight into the joys of quilt making and has taught workshops in the Southern Appalachian region. She has developed her own time-saving, accurate piecing techniques. Debbie credits her background as a math teacher for her ability to create new designs from traditional patterns.